Causing a Stir

Causing a Stir

The Secret Lives & Loves of Kitchen Utensils

poems & paintings by

Prartho Sereno

Mansarovar Press
SAN ANSELMO, CALIFORNIA

Acknowledgements

Grateful acknowledgement is made to the editors of the publications in which some of these poems and paintings first appeared: *Rosebud* and *Viha Connection*.

And affectionate thanks to my designer, the incomparable Angelina/DP, who has woven a beautiful whole from so many parts. Special thanks also to my little writing conclave: Bill Keener, Mike Day, Kathy Evans, Anila and Elianne who pored over line-break and comma, rhythm and meaning; and to Stephen and Bob at Browser Books, whose enthusiasm for the emerging project sustained me through the many hours of making. Thanks to the Fruit Medley in all its incarnations: Adina, Agnes, Anila, Aria, Elianne, Madiro, and Nirmal, for their cajoling and deep listening; and to Christine, who cheered me to splash on. Thanks to Savita for scolding me when I was about to quit after the first painting. A hugely deserved thank you to Deanna, Sandy & Mike of American Draft Source for their kindness and perseverance in the unwieldy scanning process. And thanks to all who have inspired me, many of whose spirits enchant these pages: Quincy & Nautica, Jazmine & Brandon, Drisana & Charles, Angelina, Terry, Greg & Dad, Mary, Elianne, Satprem, Kathy, Karen, Margie, Anila & Adina, Julia, Jim Guinan, Sid & Abhi, Satya Priya, Megan & Maya, Jashan, Bodhi & Bibi, Laughing Sarito, Ramakumar, and Jane's kitchen. And to Dennis who endured the whole wild ride, washing countless dinner dishes, getting me out to the beach or for a walk around the lake, and who continues to laugh at my jokes, even the works in progress.

Mansarovar Press | 5 Sierra Avenue, San Anselmo, CA 94960
www.prarthosereno.com

ISBN: 978-0-9797439-0-0
Library of Congress Control Number: 2007930968

Cover design by Angelina Sereno
www.skyboxcreative.com
Printed in China on Acid-Free Paper

for Drisana & Angelina

who have inspired me
since the days they were born

Contents

Preface

I was happy to wake to rain this morning, to sit at the breakfast table and watch the sky go from indigo to nickel-plated. The hush of the drops, the pale green of April. The warm, bighearted kitchen. In spite of her tiny dimensions and cluttered shelves, she's the roomiest place in the house. Like the kind old woman in the folk tales, however many guests come by, she always has room for more.

And the rain does what it always does – nudges us a little deeper inside, down to where the stillness lives. And if we're lucky, like I am today, we can linger inside and listen to the small voices that gravitate toward stillness, to the storytellers and poets, the Keepers of the Kitchen. You'll find them warming their hands around a cup of tea, watching the colors change beyond the window. They know nothing of hurry; theirs is all the time in the world.

These are the spirits who wrote this book. It is filled with their kind of rainy-day, teacup-in-hand Time . . . which is the domain of poetry. When I teach poems to children, I bring one out to show them. "What does this page have more of than most other pages of writing?" I ask.

It takes a while sometimes, but finally someone calls out, "Space!"

And I sigh and say, "Yes." That's what I love most about poetry – all that space. All that emptiness. A page of poetry says, "Leave the crowded world behind. Stop a while and be with me. Take your time."

Because the world has become so crowded with things to get and do and be, and because our warp-speed momentum is so difficult to stop, I have painted windows into a slower, time-rich world that hides behind our own. These windows are wide open, inviting you to kick off your shoes and climb in.

Come inside and meet the curious beings that live here. Some might seem strangely familiar. Some may seem surprisingly like *you!* I was surprised myself when I met them. It seemed they'd always been with me. And while I was painting them and writing their poems, a bit of the Kitchen's generosity began to seep into me. I began to see how every one is needed: the sharp wit of the grapefruit spoon, the straight spine of the dinner knife, the dance of the salad servers among the leaves.

It has been almost four years since the Soup Spoon first spoke to me. Then the Fork, the Teaspoon, the Knife. Each coming forward in its own time, taking me in, entrusting me with its story.

When I finished the last painting a few weeks ago, I went into the kitchen and made soup. Gathered the onions and peas, carrots and celery, parsley and thyme. I chopped and poured and sang and stirred. It was a friendly world in which I worked. So ordinary. So magic.

Now my work is done. I leave you in the capable hands of the kitchen's citizenry and with a welcoming stanza from Wise Woman Ladle:

Come to the table, empty yourself.
Set out your bowl.

Prartho Sereno
April 11, 2007
San Anselmo, California

The Lord lives among pots and pans.

—Teresa of Avila

Dinner Fork

He coined the phrase *Dig in!* –
our upright, uptight, man of steel.
Devoted worker, never makes it
back to the drawer, camps instead
all night in the drainer. But in those
moonlit hours, he sometimes wishes
for a different life.

Not that he minds shouldering
a little extra weight. He's glad
to be strong and direct. It's just that
once in a while a soufflé comes along
that puts his head in the clouds for days.

And then there's the story of Uncle Felix,
who went for a picnic and never came back.
He pictures his uncle in a bed of flowers
among the frogs and bees,
drunk on rainwater and shooting stars.

Yes, behind that stalwart stance,
the dinner fork is a dreamer.
Every winged fancy flocks
to roost in those long tines,
and they tangle there, hopelessly,
like spaghetti.

Teaspoon

No wonder the magicians
choose her to bend
with their minds.
She's the yielding one –
the Silver Queen of Yes.
Always out to lunch
or brunch, off on a picnic
or dawdling over tea.
She's everyone's sweetheart,
an inspired taker
of plunges and leaps.

Her taste for all things
tart and sweet has led her
into every kind of affair –
through terraced tea fields
and jungle plantations,
through every door that opens
to the poet's heart.

Be still sometimes
and listen
to the little sonatas
she makes at the edge
of teacup or bowl.
Her bell-like voice
will ring back the mystery,
lighten your heaviest load.

Soup Spoon

If you listen, you might hear her laughing
up there, grandmother of the top drawer.
Laughing about the way life slipped from her
like a chicken noodle. In another time
she was the bright-eyed floozy of the dining room,
but her heart was too big, she gave it all away.
Now she spends long hours in the crumb-lined corner,
remembering her days with the delft blue plate –
how they ran away together and caused
such a stir, the cook jumped over the moon.

But he was fragile, the delft blue, fell to pieces
at a family bash, leaving her alone. Oh, she's
had her flings since then – taken out to serve
rice and beans or lift the green from an avocado.
And one autumn she went to the garden
to make holes for a hundred tulip bulbs.
But in recent years it's the grandchildren –
their small hands reaching for her on rainy afternoons.
She still gives all she has, her tarnished face
beneath the golden broth – a mirror to soften our world.

Dinner Knife

Of clean line
and simple design,
straight
as the unbent arrow,
the Prince
of Understatement
stands cool
and tall
in the kitchen's heat.
Balanced
and flexible,
relaxed
and versatile,
he's almost
amphibious –
as at home
slathering jam
as slicing
through crepes.
He goes willingly
to the task at hand:
pries the lid,
tightens the screw,
taps the wineglass
to hush us all.
And once
in a dream
I took him up a ladder
to unhinge
the moon.

Butter Knife

In his previous incarnation, the butter knife
was a set of bangles on the arm of a rich,
sad woman. He was dedicated in his role
but could not cheer her – neither with jingle nor shine.

At night on her bed-stand he would fall into prayer:
Next time make me practical, something
straightforward, non-frivolous and lean.

Eventually she pawned him, as even rich women,
if they're sad enough, will do. And so he was set
to be melted and cast into the plainest knife.
But as the flames warmed him, he thought out loud:
Even if my mistress never had a glimmer,
there are those who are cheered
by the grace of a curving thing.

The silversmith heard him and said *Yes*,
because the silversmith only knows yes.

And so he was cast with a silver rose,
subtle curves of handle and blade, and given
the congenial life – passed from hand to hand,
the first, warm round of every festive affair.

Salad and Dessert Forks

The salad and dessert forks are identical twins –
perpetual teenagers in buzz cuts and baggy pants.
Quick-witted and girl-crazy, they never
stick around for a whole meal, know nothing
of soup or nuts, Beef Wellington or *coq au vin*.
Raised in a family of party-minded serving pieces,
these freewheeling forks catch what they can
around leftovers and midnight snacks.

But between themselves they've learned
to share, to trade places and balance a sweet-tooth
with cravings for greens. Their only quarrel:
who does dessert when Grandpa comes to dine.
Not because of the lemon pie, but because his stories
dazzle so. Even Auntie B doesn't jump for the dishes,
so the lucky twin gets to lie in the candlelight,
swashbuckling heroes sailing his uncharted seas.

Slotted Spoon

The slotted spoon is not oversensitive or sloppy.
She simply knows the sorcery of tears.

Understands that they should be shed
in all seasons, under all phases of the moon.

She wastes no time postponing, doesn't wait
for the grand finale of loss or gain.

Whatever she is given, she takes with an open hand
and gives back tears. And she never goes hungry.

Without begging, the essential appears in her bowl.
She is grateful, the slotted spoon, with her die-cut pattern

of rose-bud or acorn. She knows she is blessed.
Hold her face to the window and you will see the light.

Grapefruit Spoon

All dressed up with no place to go.

The grapefruit spoon is fed up

with the recent hoopla over *Simplicity*

struttin' its stuff with a capital S.

The declutter movement

has devastated the sisterhood,

depositing them like orphans

at second-hand stores.

Now it's the paring knife

and any old teaspoon – a disgrace

to the very concept of charm.

The world has lost yet another

elegant one-trick pony.

But the bigger waste is that brilliant mind

lying fallow, the cutting edge of wit

and wisdom, without which the world

is a duller place.

Pickle Fork

His mother, a pewter serving fork

and Grande Dame of the wooden platter,

warned him: *Keep eating like that*

and you'll wind up nothing

but silver and bone. And that's

pretty much the way it happened.

The pickle fork is the quintessential

picky eater, a barely-there, livin'-on-air

kind of guy. And ever since

the iced tea spoon broke his heart,

he's been a kind of daredevil,

diving headlong into the brine.

If you put your ear in his direction,

you'll hear him crooning

his vinegary love songs,

singing about her satin face

and delicate pirouettes,

her impenetrable wintry heart.

Iced Tea Spoon

You can't trust the gossip
of cold shoulders
and an icy touch.
Look into her patina'd face
and watch the bittersweet
      ballerina whirl.
Then you'll know –
      all she's ever wanted
         was to dance.

She arrived in this world
with a single purpose,
and that was to turn,
to come full circle
      again and again.
Like a compass
      or a clock.
         Like a windmill.
Like the sky with all its stars.

Measuring Spoons

This little band of gypsies
is a caravan of women in love
with the color and fragrance
of all the world.
Tuned to the earth's dark gifts –
seed pods and tree bark,
root and leaf – they bend
over backward to bring you
the mysteries that speak
to the back of your tongue.

You say weed, they say *exotic!*
You say *wild flower*, they say
saffron! You say small,
insignificant leaves; they say *coriander,*
peppermint, basil! You say *bean*,
they say, *vanilla!*
They come bearing oils, honey,
and molasses. They come making music.
Take them out and they will sing
of the wonders a spoonful can bring.

Pastry Blender

To master the art of crumble,

the way of tenderness,

let yourself teeter and tumble,

rock with your worries, roll with your stress.

Turn your mealy-mouthed mumbles

into joyful jumbles – cobblers,

tarts, Quiche Lorraine.

Never mind all the prattle

of money and fame.

Ride loose in the saddle,

be loose with the reins.

Some will taunt and call you flaky –

just say yes and take a bow.

For soon will come the *oohs* and *wows*

as it melts like butter in their mouths.

Wooden Spoons

Be glad for your wooden spoons,
whether they live on the counter
in pastoral bouquets or as urban dwellers
of the gadget drawer,
wedged between sifter and grater.

Be glad as they grow worn
and stained through the years.
For if you stand by them,
they will lead the way
through the clattering world
on moccasined feet.

These silent ones are wise
beyond their bowls;
they bear memories not their own.
Stories whisper in their veins
of maple and pine, rivers and seasons,
cycles of flood and drought.

It is a mystery even to them
why they yearn toward the window,
up through the branches,
toward the songs of calling birds
who seem, somehow, to know them by name.

Sugar Spoon

Venus on the Half Shell,

the sugar spoon rises

from a sea of blinding light,

finds herself alone,

unable to remember

where she came from

or who brought her

to this shimmering world.

Star-struck urchin,

adrift in your porcelain canoe,

you may be a stranger

in this strange land,

but you are not alone.

There are many of us here –

startled and agog

by the sweetness

we find each day

in our bowls.

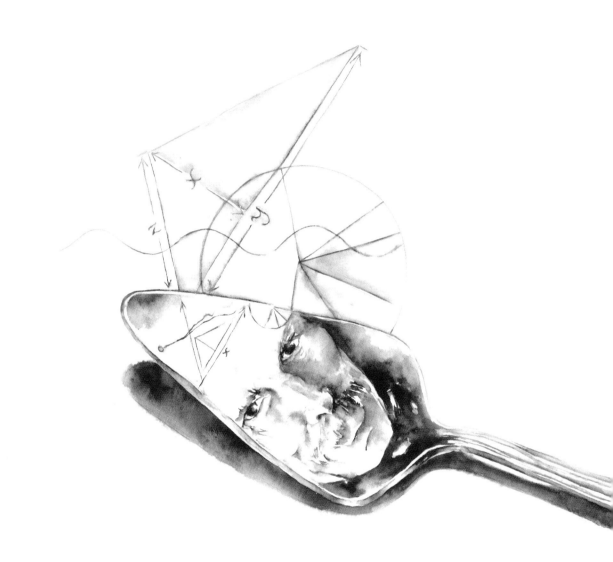

Pie Server

No matter that he takes the cake,
he's not the party animal
we've made him out to be.
No. Deep down, the pie server
is a nerd. Precision incarnate, he does
triangles around us all, can grasp
the pie chart in a single glance.

Which is not to say the girls
aren't crazy for him. Something
so enchanting about the brainy type.

But he doesn't seem to notice.
So clear about his purpose, our King
of Focus, Master of All Things Round.

It's likely he'll live out his days
as a bachelor – unfettered,
unattached. For he's the only one
who took to heart
the Ancient One's advice:
Your work is to find your work,
and then give yourself to it.

Ice Cream Scoop

You have to be open,

round and deep,

to hold a bowl of winter

in your hands.

You must gather yourself

inside your hooded cloak.

Become strong as steel

and resolute.

For one day you will be taken

to the holy rivers: Peaches

and Cream, Cocoa-Loco,

Pistachio-Pomegranate Dream.

A mysterious hand

will push you in, instruct you

to bring back something

sweet and rich. Trusting you

to add a new note

to the cool, smooth hum of the world.

Tea Ball

A fragrance is released when the soul

falls through the world, finds herself

at the bottom – the memory of something

aromatic and strong awakening inside.

The tea ball knows this.

She knows how to let go, how to wait

until everything around her is infused

with her own forgotten grace.

When you are cold and lonely,

she is the one to choose, the one

with whom you can linger

in the soothing eddies, and steep.

Spatula

A little flippant,
flipped-out and flirtatious,
the spatula comes by his bravado honestly.
Used to be with the circus:

high wire
           &   e
             t   z
           r   e
            a   p

Loves to brag about the omelets he's flipped
and the eggs he's fried, likes to kiss and tell
about his flapjack girlfriends.

Sure, he's a bit over the Big Top,
but who else can fling those patties
with the grace of a tiger,
    the balance of a juggler on a rolling globe,

            a cannon?
          from
      shot
   the dazzle of a man

Yes, he has something to teach us, the spatula –
showman, hard worker, and all-round
happy guy, keeper
   of the alchemical secret
     of changing work to play.

Barbeque Fork & Basting Brush

He's a cowboy, who's never felt at ease

with his life in the drawer – corralled there

amidst the chatter of the other forks,

their endless obsessions with the spoons.

Not that he's beyond romance; just that

he devoted himself years ago

to the basting brush, a long-handled blonde.

Her artistry still moves him, her painterly grace.

And she loves him

in his discontent, which she considers divine.

She has watched him do the fire-walk,

burn through untold troubles and fears.

Watched him rustle up potatoes and ribs,

her sentimental cowpoke of the range.

My Turning Fork, the Cook had called him,

and what she'd always known was revealed:

Everything is in the turning.

Pasta Server

It's easy, he whispers
as he enters the morass.
Take what is given,
give what is needed.

Easy is right. Right, easy.
This is what the
pasta server knows.
He knows the natural flow

of all things wet and wild –
curly noodles and fettuccini,
pasta in pesto and angel hair.
Into the thick of it he dives.
Into the tangle
that befuddles us all.

See how he neither rejects
nor grasps – happily empty,
happily full. And see:
fear has no hold on him.

Chinese Soup Spoon

The Porcelain Princess has always spoken little

and understood much. Perhaps because the potter,

when he formed her from clay,

hid the secret of friendship inside her:

Take everything with a few grains of rice.

Whisk

If the magic has fallen from your life
and you find yourself walking
the dotted lines of linear thought,
living as if you've seen the movie
and know which way the story ends . . .

If you find yourself thinking,
for example: *Water is water – liquid,*
swimmable, blue – and you've forgotten
the sloth of bear-shaped clouds
lumbering overhead. Or how you slid
on your feet across the lake last winter.
Or how the ocean is really a fire,
reducing everything to its ashes of sand.

If you find yourself thinking:
An egg white is an egg white –
transparent and gelatinous, clinging
to the bottom of the bowl . . .
it's time to have a dance with the whisk.

Whirling Dervish of the kitchen,
he knows the secret of breath and spin.
Go with him to the egg whites, watch
them rise and turn to white-capped seas.
Then watch again as the waves stand still,
turn to mountains you can move –
to a slab of ice cream or lemon pie.
Create together a brave new world,
a snowy landscape that for its final act
will disappear.

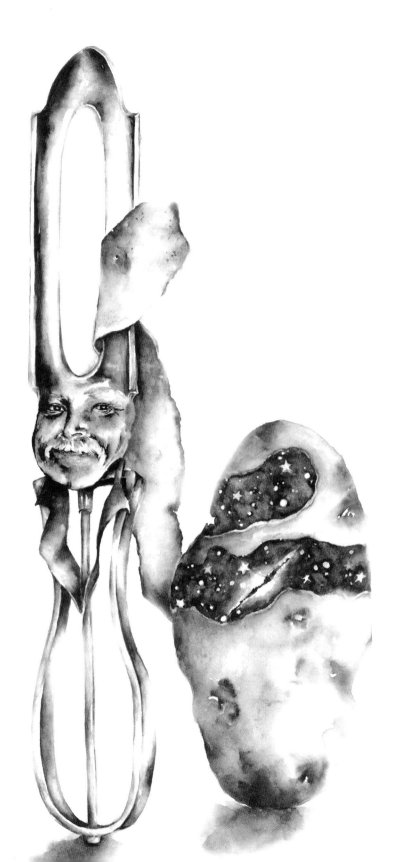

Potato Peeler

We're all helpless
in his presence.
Each glance
takes something away:
pretense, mask,
the tough skin
you took pride in.

Our coverings
become so frail
under his
haunting eye.
Be prepared to lose
everything
you think you are.

Ah, but behold the sky
of your Original Face.

Salad Servers

The salad fork and spoon are emissaries
from the lost realm of harmony.
Man and woman, together and alone.
Unalterably different – she
with her moon-roundness, her heart
a hollow place yearning to be filled.
And he, with his urge to grasp,
to move the green world, to lift it into the air
and place it before the guest.

Yes, from time to time the salad spoon
wonders why the fork can't be
a little more like her – patient,
waitful, receptive. But then she feels him
reaching out, stirring up fragrance
and light. And then she remembers
what illuminates their tango in the leaves –
opposites in completion. Night and day,
give and take, yin and yang.

L. Zester & the Squeezers

Lemon Zester, Citrus Squeezer,

Cheese Grater, Garlic Press –

the bohemian minstrels know

how to take it slow, how to s-q-u-e-e-z-e

the juice

      from root and rind.

Zip, squish, rat-a-ma-splat.

They'll help you get down,

get with it, get hip – savor the flavor

of life on the tip

      of your tongue.

Ladle

At the edge of the stove, inside the thicket
of wooden spoons and serving ware,
the Wise Woman sits. Patient.
Unperturbed. Whole.

Sister of the sundial, cousin to the wheel,
daughter of the ancient hollowed-out gourd.
Some say her greatest grandmother was born
of the Big Bang. Look north, they say,
and see her face echoed in the stars.

But look also to the ground: Rice and onion,
salt and bone. Yes, she is made of stardust,
but she can bring us back to the earth
from which we were made.

Come to the table, empty yourself.
Set out your bowl.